A Crocodile's Teeth

And Other Funny Poems by Colin West

WALKER BOOKS
AND SUBSIDIARIES
LONDON · BOSTON · SYDNEY · AUCKLAND

First published as *Height of Absurdity*
in 2005 by Walker Books Ltd
87 Vauxhall Walk, London SE11 5HJ

This edition published 2007

2 4 6 8 10 9 7 5 3 1

© 2005, 2007 Colin West

The right of Colin West to be identified as author/illustrator
of this work has been asserted by him in accordance with
the Copyright, Designs and Patents Act 1988

This book has been typeset in ITC Garamond

Printed and bound in Great Britain by
Creative Print and Design (Wales)

British Library Cataloguing in Publication Data:
a catalogue record for this book is available from the British Library

ISBN 978-1-4063-1210-2

www.walkerbooks.co.uk

Dedication

To Caroline, Caz and Hannah,
To Hannah and Caroline, Caz,
Who helped with this book in a manner
That nothing's more wonderful as.

Contents

Introduction

If, as I write
this rhyme tonight,
something should cause
my pen to pause,
it's not that I'm
bereft of rhyme,
but rather that
my sleepy cat
lies on my lap
taking a nap,
and on his paws
are great big claws
which dig deep in
my tender skin
until I must
his feet adjust,
as now indeed
I feel the need
to do, so I'll
just pause awhile...

That's better — I'm
now fit for rhyme!

Is Reading Aloud...?

Is reading aloud
in this library allowed,
or is reading aloud
not allowed?

Well, reading aloud
is allowed in this library –

AS LONG AS IT
ISN'T TOO LOUD.

Choosing a Movie

Let's see a horror film tonight
and let's have one enormous fright.
Let's see *The Monster from the Deep*
and let's all lose a good night's sleep.
Let's see the beast of Frankenstein's
and let's have shivers down our spines.
Let's see a hundred gruesome ghouls
and let's all scream like frightened fools.
Let's see a ghost without a head
and let's have nightmares when in bed.
Let's see a film that's really scary
about a Yeti, big and hairy.
Or ... (not that I'm a namby-pamby)
we could see something more like *Bambi?*

Jester

Just around
the corner
is a jester
who is jesting.
He's a jestful
sort of jester
who is just
around the corner.

The Truce

I've got a brother, name of Bruce,
and Bruce and I have formed a truce.
It's peaceful now – we never fight,
as once we did, with all our might –

we used to biff,
we used to boff,
and tear each
other's
T-shirt off.
We used to pinch,
we used to punch,
and didn't even
stop for lunch.

We used to scream,
we used to scratch,
we used to love
a boxing match.

We used to thwack,
we used to thump,
we used to bash,
we used to bump.
We used to spit,
we used to spat,
we used to knock
each other flat.

We used to butt,
we used to bite,
oh boy! how we
enjoyed a fight!

But now we don't,
we've formed a truce,
we never fight,
not me and Bruce.
We play apart
and seldom meet,
the truce is working
out a treat.

And yet when all
is said and done,
we used to have
a lot more FUN.

Family Jewels

Simon
is a rough diamond,
his little girl a pearl.
His wife's a peril
whose name is Beryl,
but his granny's
good as gold.
His baby, Ruby,
is OK, maybe
(but she's only
six months old).
His mum's a gem
and all of them
live at the top
of a jeweller's shop
in Amethyst Broadway,
London W.6.

Sailor

A sailor to the jungle-o
Retired, and built a bungalow.
He kept some sheep and cattle-o
Till off he had to shuffle-o
To make way for a buffalo,
Poor, miserable ex-matelot!

A Tale of Two Turnips

Said Mr Turnip to his wife:
"I'm growing tired of country life,
O let's away without delay
And root ourselves in London clay."

So Mr Turnip and his spouse
That night, they left their humble house,
And went forthwith to Hammersmith
And camped beneath a monolith.

And Mr Turnip and his missus
Gave each other goodnight kisses,
And slept till dawn, then all forlorn,
They walked around for half the morn.

Said Mrs Turnip to her hubby:
"My! The city streets are grubby!
And furthermore, my feet are sore –
I much preferred our life before."

So Mr Turnip and his wife,
They turned away from city life,
And took the track that led them back
To their little country shack.

Now Mr Turnip and his wife
Once more enjoy the country life,
But sometimes they are apt to say
How they liked London – for a day.

Mortar and Pestle

When it comes to a mortar and pestle
I'm never sure which one's the vessel
And which one's the thing you grind up with.
Tell me, which of the two I'd wind up with
If I went in a shop for a mortar?
Would they sell me a thing to hold water,
Or something with which I could wallop
A substance (if only a dollop)?

Conversely, if ever I bought a
Pestle, opposed to a mortar,
Would I find that I'd purchased a truncheon,
Or something to hold a small luncheon?
This riddle of mortar and pestle
Is something with which I now wrestle.

 # Ten Little Birdies

Ten little birdies
Upon a washing line…
Along came a man with a rifle,
And then there were … eight.

Eight?
Well, the gun belonged to Uncle Harold
And happened to be double-barrelled.

Adolphus

Adolphus wasn't known to swear
Or pull his little sister's hair,
Or dance upon
his granny's grave,
Or generally misbehave.
He didn't fib
or act uncouth
(In fact, he always
told the truth
And seemed
uncommonly refined)
His only vice:
he spoke his mind.

Adolphus, although
not a brat,
Could not be called
a diplomat,
Apt as he was
to mutter, "That
Is really such
an awful hat!"
Or, "Wow! Your
hairstyle looks
a mess!"
Or, "Isn't that
a dreadful dress?"

And if one countered,
"You're unkind!"
He sighed, "I merely
speak my mind."

Adolphus trod a line that's thin
'Twixt rashness and self-discipline,
Until one day that line he crossed
And found out to his bitter cost
Exactly how it felt to be
A victim of verbosity.

(He suffered this
sad circumstance
When visiting his
maiden Aunt's…)

To Auntie Jane he said, "That hue
Of pink you wear is most un-you.
With such a tone of skin you've got,
You shouldn't wear a pink so 'hot',
No, I don't like that pink one jot!"

How Auntie riled, she looked quite grim
And thought that she would give to him
A taste of his own medicine
(No longer could she hold it in)...

"You horrid and obnoxious child.
Your lack of tact quite drives me wild.
And even though you may be young,
You should know when
to hold your tongue.

Too long I've suffered from your scorn,
Right from the moment you were born,
When first you hollered at the midwife,
You've caused the crisis of my midlife
Nephew! How you make me ill!
I'll cut you forthwith from my will!"

For once the boy was lost for speech
(His Auntie was extremely rich).
He wishes now he'd not expressed
A view on how the lady dressed
And had, instead, been disinclined
To rashly go and speak his mind.

The Vanishing

After vanishing:
a bottle, and a bunny,
and a hankie, and some money,
The Mighty Marvo took his book
of spells down from the shelf,
and vanished …
himself.

Now we can't touch or hear him,
and though we feel near him,
no more can we see him.
Oh will the spell free him one day?
Or will it forever bind him?
Will we ever find him,
or *has* he been magicked away?

Boysenberries

"Boysenberries,
boysenberries,"
cried
the foreigner
gladly.

"Poison berries,
poison berries,"
sighed
the coroner
sadly.

Big Top Topics

The funambulist mumbles:
"This really is fun!"
But if his foot stumbles –
He's done.

The acrobat's talents
May cut quite a dash,
But if he's off-balance –
He'll crash.

The fire-eater wallows
In fame coast-to-coast,
But if the chap swallows –
He's toast.

The trapeze artist reckons
His antics enthrall,
But if his grip slackens –
He'll fall.

The lion tamer's plucky
And looks pleased
as Punch,
But if he's not lucky –
He's lunch.

Though daredevil workers
Sure bring the house down,
I'll stay in the circus –
A clown.

Food for Thought

Some people make a lot of fuss
when asked to eat asparagus,
whilst others stubbornly decline
fine caviar when out to dine,
and others still will holler "No"
when dished up eels or escargots.
Such things in mind, is this OK,
a burger from the takeaway?

A Crocodile's Teeth

A crocodile's teeth are a problem,
a crocodile's teeth are a pain.
A crocodile suffers the toothache
again and again and again.

Now, getting the toothache so often,
makes crocodiles lose all their bite,
and desperate measures are called for
to bring back their lost appetite.

Thus crocodiles go to the dentist
on average, every eight years.
(Quite by chance, that's precisely how often
a dentist, somewhere, disappears.)

I Read my Book

I read my book
with the radio on.
The music played,
the music won.

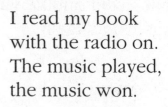

I read my book
in front of the TV.
A page an hour
it took me.

I read my book
at night in bed.
It sent me to sleep,
so I dreamt instead.

I read my book
beneath a tree.
I met two beetles
and a bee.

I read my book
when on the train,
but gazed out the window
again and again.

I read my book
while having tea,
and didn't glance
at Chapter Three.

So...
I went to my room
and read my book
in silence.
I read my book,
I read my book,
I read my book,
I read my book.
I went to my room
and read my book,
I read my book
in silence.

My Teacher

My teacher doesn't bellow,
My teacher doesn't shout,
She doesn't lose her temper
Or wave her arms about.
My teacher's always smiling,
My teacher's always kind,
And always in good humour,
But only in my mind.

Teachers

Some are good, and some are bad,
and some are in-between.
Some are fat, and some are thin,
and some are in-between.
Some are polite, and some are rude,
and some are in-between.
Some are kind, and some are mean,
and some are in-between.

N.B. The above poem can also be applied to:
bank managers, footballers, school children,
policemen, poets, bishops, window-cleaners, etc. etc.

Coathanger

I gave my love a coathanger.

She flung it back at me.

It acted like a boomerang, and hit her on the knee.

The Ghoulish Gazette

Gothic manor for sale.

Extensive dungeon with en-suite torture chamber. Potential for expansion. Needs some modernization. Phone Flogborough 666 after midnight.

House trained dragons

for sale. Make excellent pets. Also ideal as alternative central heating. Phone Mumblethorpe 6749.

Headless giant

seeks attractive giantess (over 20 stone), view to marriage and setting up Charm School. P.O. Box 721, Throttlewaite.

Wanted urgently

by animal lover: bats, newts, frogs and toads. Also large cauldron. Will collect. Phone Uggleton 3819.

Young-at-heart ghost

(aged 341) seeks ghostess (aged 280–320) for romantic graveyard strolls and chain-rattling sessions. Apply Cobblestone Cottage, Tingle-down-the-Spine.

Easy-going ogre
seeks lodgings.
Good cook,
fond of children.
Phone Grimbleton 7318.

Reliable phantom
seeks night work
in or around Highgate.
Frightening unwelcome
guests a speciality.
Enquire Cemetery Gates
(ask for Cyril).

Lost:
one scrawny black cat,
answers to name of
Igor.
Left ear missing,
vile nature,
vicious snarl.
Much missed.
Reward offered
for safe return...
Cobweb Cottage,
Hobble-on-the-Hill.

For sale:
one broomstick.
Hardly used.
Will consider exchange
for lady's bicycle.
Phone Aldwitch 9352.

Wanted
One hundred vampires
for research by large
false teeth factory
Send details to:
Head Office
Toothypeg Ltd.,
Tooting Bec.
No personal callers.

**Don't forget to
mention the Ghoulish
Gazette when
answering any advert.
FANGS A LOT!**

The Sighs of Simon Sage

"When reading books," sighed Simon Sage,
"'Tis such a dreadful bore
To have to, time and time again,
Turn every spent page o'er.
O, could that I but find someone
To rid me of this chore."

A passing student chanced to hear
The sighs of Simon Sage,
And offered free of charge to be
The Turner of the Page.
So Simon took him up on it –
But gave the boy a wage.

Silent Letters

Two silent letters are K and G
in knot and gnome and gnat and knee.
Another unpronounced is P
in psalm and in psychology.
And one more still is W
when found in wrist and wrinkle too.
Remember, then, there's just a few
weird words like knock and wreck and gnu.

14½

They've gone and built
a house between
Numbers Fourteen
and Sixteen,
and called it (and
it makes me laugh)
Number Fourteen-
and-a-half.

I wondered who'd
want such a place
in such a tall
and narrow space,
and so I walked
up to the door
to look more closely
and I saw

upon a plaque
engraved with care,
the name of who'd
be moving there
(at Number Fourteen-
and-a-half)
the name was
Mr A. G. Raffe.

Adrian

Has everyone met Adrian?
He really is a hoot.
I gave a birthday party –
So he wore his birthday suit.

And when he played his trumpet
It was wonderful to hear –
He didn't put it to his lips,
But played the thing by ear.

And then he babysat for us,
And acted just as daft:
He sat upon the baby
And he laughed and laughed
and laughed.

O, if you should meet Adrian,
And say, "How do you do?"
"How do I do precisely what?"
Is what he'll ask of you.

Lion Cloth

To swap my life with Tarzan's
I would give a golden coin –
I'd put that funny loin cloth on
To cover up my loin.

I'd also need a *lion* cloth
In case one day I met
A lion in the jungle whom
I fancied as a pet.

I'd lie my trusty lion cloth down
And wait for him to tread

Somewhere upon the middle, when
I'd whack him on the head.

I'd gather up the corners then
And with him knocked out cold,
I'd take the bundle back to Jane,
Which she could then unfold.

Imagine Jane's delight when she
Espied the dozy cat
A-sitting on my lion cloth
As though it were a mat!

Magic Me This

Magic me this,
and Magic me that,
a new bell and collar
for Kitty my cat.

Magic me that,
and Magic me this,
a frog who's awaiting
a princess to kiss.

Magic me this.
and Magic me that,
a new broom to fly
on at night like a bat.

Magic me that,
and magic me this,
then long will I cackle
and Kitty will hiss.

A Dog

A dog as friend
is tops.

A dog as playmate,
likewise.

But going on a cycle ride,
A dog's a nuisance
bikewise.

Fergus MacPherson

This is the story of Fergus MacPherson,
a normal and ordinary sort of a person,
who's neither too short and who's neither too tall,
there's nothing unusual about him at all.

He hasn't green hair
that he wears as a thatch,
where parrots can sit
on their eggs till they hatch.
He hasn't a cat
that he's teaching to grunt
or even a horse
that he rides back to front.

He's never been
up in a bicycle plane,
or travelled at night
on a crocodile train.

No, Fergus MacPherson
has done nothing much,
he just tends to water
his garden and such.

But once, when he noticed his birthday was near,
he thought he would make it a memorable year:
"I'll do something strange that I never have done,"
he vowed to himself, "and it might be good fun!"

So Fergus went down
to Loch Ness for a swim,
but nothing incredible
happened to him.
And as he went home,
Fergus thought:

"Oh, my word, again nothing
out of the normal's occurred."

And that was the story of Fergus MacPherson,
a normal and ordinary sort of a person,
who's neither too short and who's neither too tall,
there's nothing unusual about him at all.

Feeble Excuses

I'll do it Sunday.
I'll do it Monday.
I'll do it one day,
Promise.

I'd really like to.
I'd dearly like to.
I'd clearly like to,
But...

Then suddenly,
It was too late.

I could've done it.
I should've done it.
I would've done it,
If only...

Memories

Memories of holidays ... and fun.
Memories of happy days ... and un-.
Memories of Saturdays ... and Sun.
Memories of yesterdays ... long gone.

Memories are what is left
When all the doing's done.

A Crusty Loaf of Bread

Into the supermarket
walks little Winifred:
she's just popped in to purchase
a crusty loaf of bread.
But soon she starts to notice
what's on the nearest shelf:
"Mmm ... that looks
rather tempting,"
she mutters to herself.

So she takes down a packet
of cornflakes, and then spies
a "super special" offer
on oven-ready pies.
She picks a Steak and Kidney,
then suddenly she sees
her favourite sort of yoghurt
next to the eggs and cheese.

So Winnie gets her yoghurt,
some cheddar and some brie,
then half a dozen farm eggs
to have for Sunday tea.
And then around the corner
along another aisle,
she stops before the biscuits
for just a little while.

Then come the crisps and peanuts,
she gets some, then some dates,
and then a tube of Smarties
and a box of After Eights.
Then Winnie wheels her trolley
towards the marmalade,
and on the way she stocks up
with lime and lemonade.
Then as she's glancing sideways,
she sees a big display
of sardines, so she gets some:
"They're ten pence off today!"

Next Winnie sees there's plenty
of lovely looking greens,
so Winnie picks a cabbage,
some brussels sprouts and beans.
And then she gets bananas,
and pears and tangerines,
and kiwi fruits and melons
and grapes and aubergines.

Now Winnie's been an hour,
and though she's yet to find
quite what she came inside for,
she doesn't seem to mind,
For nearby is the cake stand,
she picks a marzipan,
an apple tart, a jam roll,
and then a cherry flan.

And though her trolley's heavy,
still Winnie ventures on –
she can't resist a bargain
before it might be gone.
So when she spots a notice
"Quick – buy one, get one free",
she adds a pair of kippers
and smiles with fiendish glee.

And then, all of a sudden,
at last, the loaves of bread.
She chooses one that's crusty
and joins the queue ahead.
But waiting there, she picks up
a Twix and Milky Way,
and one such bar as helps you
to work and rest and play.

Now Winnie's at the check-out,
she goes to buy her stuff.
She turns out all her money,
but hasn't quite enough.

I'll have to put back something,
thinks worried Winifred.
So what does Winnie leave behind?
The crusty loaf of bread!

Loops of Tape

I wish I knew the person who
Somewhere just sits and sews
Those little loops of tape inside
The collars of our clothes.

For if I knew that person, then
I'd say to him, "Hey, look,
My loop is broke and I can't hang
My coat up on the hook."

Allegate

There's no such word as 'allegate',
but what am I to do?
An angry alligator
that I met at London Zoo
is making allegations
that my theory is untrue.

My Bike

I like
My bike:
Its gears and its brakes,
The noise that it makes
When I go ting-a-ling
On the thing
Called its bell.

I adore
Even more
How it feels
When its wheels
Spin around and around
Wherever is found
A deep dell.

The thrill
Of a hill
When descending at speed
Is enthralling indeed,
Although as we know,
Things don't always go
Too well:

Last week
From a peak
I coasted, and put
My left foot
In a spoke –
My collarbone broke
When I fell.

Beverly

I'm glad I'm not like Beverly
who studies Economics.

Her time she uses cleverly
but I like reading comics!

Bartholomew

The way in which Bartholomew
Pranced with his croquet mallet
Showed that he was a gentleman –
And one who liked the ballet.

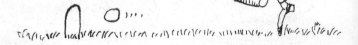

Smellyvision

Have you heard of smellyvision?
It's just like television
except as well as sight and sound,
different smells abound.

What fun!
Imagine – we switch on
"Gardening Time" on BBC2,
and not only do we hear and view
a programme on roses –
but we find the smells go right up our noses!

A million people, I bet,
would sit by a smellyvision set
to sample the experts talking of blooms
which emitted aromas right into their rooms,
but I suppose there'd be rather fewer
when those gardening experts got on to manure.

If...

If you're hanging from a clifftop
with the fingers of one hand,
and you start to think about it,
but you cannot understand
why on earth your expeditions
do not go the way you've planned,
don't be concerned, just be prepared
to very shortly land.

And don't be solemn,
don't be sad,
just think of all
the fun you've had!

If you're stranded on an iceberg
and your winter clothes are few,
and you wonder why your body
has just started changing hue,
and you think about it deeply,
but you haven't got a clue,
don't be concerned, just
be prepared
to turn a shade of blue.

And don't feel bitter,
don't feel bad,
just think of all
the fun you've had!

If you're hounded by hyenas
in some horrid, torrid zone,
and you wonder for a moment
as to whether you're alone,
and you look around intently
but you find you're on your own,
don't be concerned, just be prepared
to give a dog a bone.

And don't be moody,
don't be mad,
just think of all
the fun you've had!

Martha, Maggie and Me

On Saturday, Martha and Maggie and me
rode on our bicycle fashioned for three,
with Martha before, and with Maggie behind,
and me in the middle, we went like the wind.
And what did we see? Well, it has to be said,
with Maggie behind and with Martha ahead,
that Martha great wonders before her did see,
and me, I saw Martha, and Maggie saw me.

Preposition

Informing people is my mission
just where to place a preposition.
It is a subject, there's no doubt,
we should be hearing more about.
(Or more about which we should be hearing.)
Now ... why's everybody disappearing?

A Smile Came Over his Face

A smile came over his face,
a smile came over his face,
but come to think of it,
could a smile be any other place?

59

The Ungrateful Kid

At Christmas time it's such a bore
To get a gift one's had before.
That such a thing occurred this year
Is why I'm lacking Yuletide cheer.

How thoughtless of old Grandmama
To send me that toy racing car,
When, on my birthday last July
My Uncle Jim (it makes me cry)

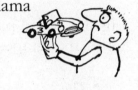

Had given me the selfsame toy.
Now, though I'm not a greedy boy
It seems to me a crying shame
To have two cars that are the same

When there are countless other things
That I'd prefer – a bird that sings,

An aeroplane, a sailing boat,
A castle with a keep and moat,

A money box, a cricket bat,
A wind-up mouse, a real live rat,

A skipping rope, a cowboy suit,
A saxophone, a drum, a flute,

A fishing rod, a pair of skates,
A bunch of grapes, a box of dates,

A yo-yo or a bouncy ball,
Yes, almost anything at all

Except a toy I've had before,
That really is the utmost bore.

And next time I see Grandmama
I'll give her back that racing car
And tell her in the future NOT
To send gifts I've already got.

Joker

I am the Joker in the pack,
The card who makes you smile.
I'm not like King or Queen or Jack,
I am the Joker in the pack –
The cheeky one who answers back
And tells you all the while:
"I am the Joker in the pack,
The card who makes you smile."

Going to Bed

Go to bed early –
Your hair grows curly.

Go to bed late –
Your hair grows straight.

Go to bed not at all –
Your hair will fall,
And you'll be bald
As a billiard ball.

Things to Throw and Catch

Think of things
that you can throw:
a stone,
a pot,
a party.
Think of things
that you can catch:
a ball,
a fish,
the measles.
A few more things
that you can throw:
your voice,
a look,
a tantrum.
A few more things
That you can catch:
a bus,
your breath,
a movie.

There's lots of things
to throw and catch –
good luck your whole life through
with all the things
in life you catch
and all life throws at you.